REJOICINGS

METRO
BOOK CO.

Los Angeles

REJOICINGS

POEMS 1966-1972

BY

GERALD STERN

Copyright © 1973 by Gerald Stern

All rights reserved.
This edition originally issued in 1984 by Metro Book Co.,
3208 Cahuenga Blvd. West, Los Angeles, Ca. 90068.

Library of Congress Catalog Card Number 83-63291
ISBN 0-915371-00-6
ISBN 0-915371-01-4 pbk.

Printed and bound in the United States of America

10 9 8 7 6 5 4 3 2 1

Some of these poems first appeared in the following magazines:
The Enigma, Parchment Conch, The Scotsman, and *The Smith,* to
whose editors acknowledgments are due.

CONTENTS

REJOICINGS

REJOICINGS

I put the sun behind the Marlborough Blenheim
so I can see the walkers settling down
to their long evening of relaxation
over the slimy piers.

I put the clouds in their place and start the ocean
on its daily journey up the sand;
I reach the beach a minute after the guards
have chased the last sleepers from their blankets.

Haley's blimp
drags its long tail across the sky
as the light from Greenland dips down
for a quick look at my broken stick.

I make a good circle before digging
so I can close the whole world in my grip
and draw my poor crumbling man
so that his tears fall within the line.

The sand, half out of focus, lightens and darkens
according to the clouds and the sun
and takes all I have of pity and fear
like a weak and devoted friend.

A few black puffs, the end of some great violence,
blow into the wind before their dispersal.
I move my lips and raise my quiet hand
in all the craziness of transferred emotion.

After twenty years of dull loyalty
I have come back one more time to the shore,
like an old prisoner—like a believer—
to squeeze the last poetry out of the rubbish.

I pour a little mud on my head
for the purification
and rub the dirty sand into my shirt
to mix everything with crystal.

I put a piece of shell for killing birds
in the open hand
and all the paraphernalia of the just,
bottle and paper and pencil,

for the work to come.
I wait one hour. That is the time it takes
to free the soul, the time it takes
for reverence.

Once or twice I have to alter the grave
so the water can come in quietly.
I am burying our Nietzsche;
I am touching his small body for the last time.

THE NAMING OF BEASTS

You were wrong about the blood.
It is the meat-eating lamb we are really terrified of,
not the meat-eating lion.
The noisy Soul shrieking and spitting and bleeding set us off—
the smell of nice clean grass confused us.
It is the eyes, it is the old sweet eyes showing just a little fear.
It is the simple mouth full of honest juices.
It is the little legs crossed at the bony joints.
—It is not greed—it can't be greed—it is fasting;
it is not divorce—it is custody;
it is not blood—it is supineness.

THIS IS LORD HERBERT MOANING

This is Lord Herbert moaning and sighing over his lost manuscripts.
This is meek old Blake wandering down the street with his wolf's face on.
Lamb, Lamb is a master—Marvell, Sidney, beautiful, beautiful,
A whole world of lucid and suffering poets talking to themselves.
I dream almost steadily now of interpenetration,
but not with beasts—I have had that for twenty years—
I begin with sanity now, I always begin with sanity.
—After a period of time the old lobster crawls back into his cave;
after a period of time the wise Indian puts on female clothes.
I watch them with love;
my own poor ghost would like to smash everything,
woods and all, cave and all;
I have to smother him with kisses,
I have to carry him from the room,
I have to show him what darkness is, what brightness is.
For twenty years, without knowing the name, I fought against beasts,
but my whole life is centered now in my lips
and their irruptions.
   It is beautiful watching the sun slip through the bent fingers.
   It is beautiful letting the brain move in and out of its own cloudbank.

IN KOVALCHICK'S GARDEN

It is dusk, the drive-ins are opening, the balloon is coming to rest.
Out of the east, so fitting, the cardinal moves into the light.
It is the female, almost too small and shabby for its splendor.
Her crest opens out—I watch it blaze up.
She is exploring the dead pear tree.
She moves quickly in and out of the dry branches.
Her cry is part wistful, part mordant.
She is getting rid of corpses.

THE BLESSED

He who destroys, he who reigns, he who meditates;
now, more than ever before, these are the three.
It is life simplifying itself,
the head cut off and the face lifted.
It is the brown rabbit dying of its fever;
it is the gray one surviving.
It is the little house of justice.
It is the dead picking flowers, dancing and eating corn.
It is the new one waving his sheaf.
It is the old one wiping his eye.
It is the Eagle Knight shaking the whole desert with his passion.
It is the strange pity of Rimbaud.
It is the strange pity of Browning. It is the towers meeting.
It is the soul of Whitehead moving into its last obscurity.
It is Walter Savage Landor's dream of entablature.
It is Walter Savage Landor in the eighteenth century.
It is Landor's hatred of kings. It is Landor's mind.
It is Landor's ceremony. It is Landor's violence.
It is the life. It is the vile reduction.
It is the new one picking flowers.
It is the old one wiping his nose, waving his eye.
It is the terror of criticism.
It is the torment of money.
It is the weariness of work.
It is the gravity of love. It is the dignity of isolation.

THE UNITY

How strange it is to walk alone,
the one leg never growing tired of the other;

the ears still beautiful but the sound
falling in new places;

all that I formerly believed in
explained and sweetened.

I have to concoct my own past now
out of old inhalations.

I have to live in two lives
with the same blood.

I have to separate the thirsts
without hatred.

It is a good desert—
snakes and horses—

cooks, whores, doctors—
ghosts, vistas,

women and men of all sizes and all ages
living together, without satire.

HIS ANIMAL IS FINALLY A KIND OF APE

His animal is finally a kind of ape—after all—and not an elephant,
a release for him, but more than that for the two exhausted beasts.
For years he struggled between them
and it was either the violence of the one or the obscurity of the other,
either way, as it seemed to him then, a concealment,
but now that the choice was made
they could move back into a simple relationship with him, and with each
      other.

What is amazing is the choice itself.
You would expect him to move from elephants into owls
or into the seal-like creatures or into pelicans,
or at least—if he had to go back—back now into hares—
or shrews and weasels, if what he needed was viciousness.
At least you would never expect him to choose the ape again,
not after three hundred years of greed and malice,
but what he was after was not the choosing of new animals
but another collaboration with the old ones,
and for this purpose the ape now more than the elephant
would suit his fever, or what there was left of it.

I remember sitting and talking for hours about the elephant.
I remember the room trembling with belief
and I hesitate, out of loyalty, to do any harm to that beast.

But it is he who will be free at last of *my* compulsion,
and able to graze, and able to panic,
without my interference.
The ape is different—it will be years before he is free;
in the meantime, when we rise we will rise for each other
and when we howl it will be in each other's faces.

There is nothing degrading or cynical in this.
We had to go back again for the sake of all three.
Otherwise we would mix our disgust forever with our dream.
What the ape does is separate once and for all the one from the other.
What he does is illuminate the distance.
What he does is make it bearable.
The leaves sticking out of his mouth, the puffed-out belly, the dirt on his
    lips,
this I pity;
the muzzled face, the musk-like odor,
this I pity.
I lived and I lived constantly on the verge of a true destruction.
Because of these animals I was able to break away.
I am in their debt.

THE GOONS ARE LEAVING

The goons are leaving, and the Hawaiians, and the taffy-pullers,
and the charred wives, and the blackmailers:
this is their Labor Day, the feast of wages.
Only the insolvents are left, and the waifs, and the vagrants.
For one more week we will move through the loose sand
in simple luxury.
We will walk into the sanctuaries and turn the signs;
we will pick our way through the wreckage;
we will start fires;
we will lie in the sun.
At night we will walk the 127 miles in peace.
We will shake the bones of the Unamis and the Presbyterians.
We will sit in the Mansion of Health.
We will rid ourselves of the consining insects.
We will smell the old meadows.
We will undress in the cedars.
We will meet raven on the beach.
Only money and luck have made us different from the others.
We live in grief and ecstasy.
It is our justice.

BIRD CURSING

For King Hoban Topatrapanning

I want to watch my sweet body go out again into the beach plums
and hang again with all that luxury
between the marsh islands of Stone Harbor
and the monkey gardens of Anglesea.

I want to see my dark shoulders rise and fall
in oblique reference to the cry of hunger
and the large shadow slipping over the lawns.

I want to hear the great grasses hiss with delight
as Wildwood drops back again into the sand.

I WILL BE A ROMANTIC

To the wild grape vine, the wild hop vine, the honeysuckle and the
    Virginia creeper
I sing my song.

When I die I will not hang under the loose pipe
or in the cellar beside the broken screens
or in the YMCA or at the Greenwich.

A gull will carry my bulging eye to a clean and brilliant place
in the fields of guano.
I will be enriched.

ON THE FAR EDGE OF KILMER

I am sitting again on the steps of the burned out barrack.
I come here, like Proust or Adam Kadmon, every night to watch the sun leave.
I like the broken cinder blocks and the bicycle tires.
I like the exposed fuse system.
I like the color the char takes in the clear light.
I climb over everything and stop before every grotesque relic.
I walk through the tar paper and glass.
I lean against the lilacs.
In my left hand is a bottle of Tango.
In my right hand are the old weeds and power lines.
I am watching the glory go down.
I am taking the thing seriously.
I am standing between the wall and the white sky.
I am holding open the burnt door.

BY COMING TO NEW JERSEY

By coming to New Jersey I have discovered the third world
that hangs between Woodbridge Avenue and Victory Bridge.
It is a temporary world,
full of construction and water holes.
full of barriers and isolated hydrants,
a world given over to Humble,
no place to live, no place to walk,
not even in hatred.
But wherever I am it has nothing anymore to *do* with hatred,
anymore than it has to do with haggling wisdom.
I live in weird equipoise, all the time now,
like a banded turkey, one foot on top of the other,
my heart jumping between two weights,
my ruined tongue reminiscing, my brain wandering.

GOING NORTH ON 202

Going north on 202 I have to wait for hours
for the American lambs to pass by.
Thousands, thousands, crossing the great circle at Flemington,
more thousands coming up the road from Frenchtown,
the meat juices running down their lips,
their undersides stained with excrement,
their hooves bloody from fighting.

On route 78 I pass Columbus
going the other way, looking for the Hudson.
His boat rocks on the empty highway
as he struggles through New Jersey.
In the back seat the cross
rattles against the window
and the frightened chickens scream.
In one more hour he will enter the last tunnel
before his departure.

With its small people standing in the rain,
with its bishops smiling happily,
with its daydreaming kings scratching their stomachs,
with its donkey races, and its monsters, and its bells,
tiny Europe waits for him,
tiny Europe, smelling of camphor.

THE POEM OF LIFE

*Why should our nation, into whose purses of charity are poured countless
dollars, permit the birds of her land, her poets, to suffer scorn and privation?*

Robert Summers, My Poem of Life

For three days now I have been watching the blue jay take over—
my soul there, shrieking and squalling,
nodding and jerking its head, fluting its tail.
All day Friday it moved nervously between the two maples.
All day Saturday it hopped through the garbage collecting wisdom.
Today it is Sunday, June 4, 1968—I have *marked* it.
My wife and Bob Summer's wife and the little stoned dancer
have driven to New York to look at Martha Graham's old age.
Summers and I are sitting under the honeysuckles
smoking parodis and discussing the poem of life.
Once he had it down to thirteen words—
the Napoleonics, the logic, the letters of pride,
the six demonstrations, the five assumptions,
all his anger and irony, all his honesty,
his dream of the theatre, his terror, his acts of power—
reduced to thirteen words.
—The blue jay is youth, right?—
clawing his chin, stuffing his belly, fighting the dove, fighting the owl,
filling the lawns and woods with his violent sounds.

By eight o'clock everything will be quiet here.
The miserable family upstairs will slam their back door,
the jays will disappear into the maples
and we will have the yard to ourselves.
We will go on for hours,
moving our lips, waving our parodis,
seizing and judging everything that comes
into the range of our brutal memories,
two delectable Jews,
spending our happy and cunning lives
in the honeysuckles.

THE WEEDS

I love the weeds—I dream about them—
grass clogging the ditches, mustard sleeping in the ground—
I love their stubbornness and secrecy.
Five years ago I thought only about a war
and like a greedy Czar
my mind was fixed on the inhuman heaven of the west;
now almost for the first time I am free of that sickness
and able to live without a constant slaughter.

The mother of violence goes in dirt and water.
She dreams of irrigation and her mouth opens at the sight of dams.
She stands like Charlemagne among the delphiniums,
crushing the Saxons and feeding the poor.
She reads the lecture on smothering to the little sons and daughters of grass.
She divides the good from the damned.

I want a king to go easily into the trees.
I want his sticks to break without horror.
I want the wind to lengthen his muscles.
I want him to despise mortification.
I want him to make a final choice between regulation and affection.
I want the water to come from his own eyes.
I want him to be carried with aplomb.
I want him to be alive.

Wind is the last master.
It blows the crazy fire, it splits the rain,
it pulls at the mind.
What is pernicious? Here in New Brunswick the dead are gluttonous.
They crowd the river. They move against the bridge.
They cross the parkway. They circle the missions. I sing
to myself like a lost Tzaddik in front of the First
Dutch Church on Neilson Street, for that is my nature;
and I walk down Little Carthage dreaming of ungoverned bodies,
for that is my nature too;
and I crowd the river myself in order to feel
the greed at its source, for that is my nature too.
Life on the earth is not a sickness. For years
I hung—like a German—between two wildernesses.
Now there is a third. I cross it with relief.

THE SUPREME SUBJECT

Pittsburgh, 1967

At an unexpected turn in the Kiskiminetas
I suddenly saw again what the valley looked like
before the Scotchman came with his bitter stick.
—It is what we spent our youth arguing over:
the beauty of the rivers before the settlement
and the horror after.
The supreme subject! Contracted in our lives!
    We talked through smoke—in Hell—like fiery puddlers,
rubbing the cinders out of our hair and spitting
out clinkers.
    It was sad, really—
we couldn't even enjoy the dreams of the Tortured,
our Hell was so literal.
Not that we were advanced. God! God!
We were just getting into the sensitive
when everyone else was moving on to the vile,
and when we looked up
our eyes were red with poverty as well as grime.

Gilbert went to Provence;
I went to Batsto;

and Hazley went to the mountain.
But what I write about—
and I think what we all write about—
is someway connected with the memory of that darkness
and our escape.

For the rest, I have no heart:
Thomas Mellon howling among the Presbyters.
Frick bleeding.
Berkman raging.
The reconciliation. The conversion.

Entelechy? The Soul?

Well, we do have interesting place names in western Pennsylvania.
Everybody knows Blueball and Intercourse down there in the East,
but we have irony, our cities are named after trees,
trees and animals, and of course millionaires, and of course Indians.
—Kiss, kiss Mamma for me. Say hello to your Mary.
Goombye, Hunkies. Goombye, goombye, Hunkies.

WHEN I HAVE REACHED THE POINT OF SUFFOCATION

When I have reached the point of suffocation,
then I go back to the railroad ties

and the mound of refuse.
Then I can have sorrow and repentance,

I can relax in the broken glass
and the old pile of chair legs;

I am brought back to my senses
and soothed a little.

It is really the only place I can go
for relief.

The streets, the houses, the institutions,
and the voices that occupy them,

are too hard and ugly
for any happiness

and the big woods outside
too full of its own death—

I go to the stone wall,
and the dirty ashes,

and the old shoes,
and the daisies.

It takes years to learn how to look at the destruction
of beautiful things;

to learn how to leave the place
of oppression;

and how to make your own regeneration
out of nothing.

MY FLOW: HIS STOPPAGE

In the next booth over the hairless white
With the shivering legs and rotten shoes
Is straining and grieving, the pain of stoppage
Acute, the pain of blockage frenzied;

His feet curling, his breath coming
In intervals, his shanks hammering
The blazed puny wooden walls
Of all three booths, in his stoppage one empty;

While I in alternate vegetable coldness
And vegetable heat and vegetable sorrow—
A vague distressing sense of sickness,
Dolor, weakness, regret, suspicion—
Am frightened more by my flow than his stoppage.

NO MERCY, NO IRONY

This is the hawk I love.
His weight is determined precisely by the distance of his fall.
He sticks to his decisions.

LOST WITH LIEUTENANT PIKE

How was I to know—in 1938—that anyone but
Zebulon Pike could be the master of my imagination·

or that the one book belonging to my dead sister—*Alice in
Wonderland*—did not have to lie for twenty years, hidden
on a closet shelf

or that I was allowed to throw out my stupid molds, my
set, that never once, with all my pouring, managed to make
one soldier without a leg missing or without an incredible
wound in the side of his neck.

Slowly I became a man, and as I did I looked back with
shame, which was the lawful payment for my ignorance and meekness.

Whatever I have to do now to outlive my string of errors I will do,
and I will live as divided as I have to, and as loose and as senseless.

In another life it will be all masted vessels and sugar houses
and tea-pouring and little men running down their lanes;
this time around there will be no government for anyone.

I have to live on the lid of Hell, poor friend;
I have to leave the woods and the Shul and the chicken

standing on its wings and the white silk scarf
and the visit from Mars and the long journey to Harrisburg, Pa.

It is something to stand on a hill in the middle of November,
9,000 miles from Jerusalem, with the ice forming
inside your nostrils, and to feel your own widsom.

GOODBYE, MORBID BEAR

Goodbye, morbid bear; you will be waving your morbid arm forever,
forcing your way into the nursery rhymes.

IMMANUEL KANT AND THE HOPI

There was a time
when the only friends I had were trees
and the only pleasure I had
was with my crippled soldiers and my glue.
I don't say this aloud
out of any sickening desire to bring back the sensitive years,
like little Lord Christ
over in the Blue House,
but only because I am spending more and more of my time remembering
as my eyes change.
I guess you should weep for me because I am thinking,
like the silk merchants of Easton in their meditation rooms,
and the dead barbers in their chairs,
and the gorillas on their stone seats.
I could spend about ten good years
bringing the things together
that go into my brain,
ten good years on the river
watching the spars and the starved deer and the bathtubs float by.
    Up the street McCormick lies in wait for me,
hoping to help me with my tires and my trees
and down the street Repsher senior burns and burns,
an abused man, living on anger.
I go in and out of this road every day now
as you do on an island.

My house, with its nine white pillars,
sits peacefully on the ground
and I am the strange man
who has moved into the ruin.
From now on I am going to have something to think about
when I drive into the parking lots;
I am going to be refreshed when I walk over the asphalt;
I am going to live on two levels, like a weasel.

It is spring; 1971.
I am looking through my open windows at the Delaware River.
I am looking through the locust trees that grow here like weeds.
This summer I am going to strip some of the delicate leaves from their stems;
I am going to swim over to Carpentersville;
I am going to write twenty poems about my ruined country.
    Please forgive me, my old friends!
I am walking in the direction of the Hopi!
I am walking in the direction of Immanuel Kant!
I am learning to save my thoughts—like
one of the Dravidians—so that nothing will
be lost, nothing I tramp upon, nothing I
chew, nothing I remember.

PLEISTOCENE

I wasn't sure—when I reached 45—
whether I would grow less and less interested in the densities
and move, like Samadryad, into the unobstructed
or whether I would begin, finally, to accept them all
one by one, in their time and at their own bidding.
To the left is the way of Lear, the penniless old man of the library,
struggling with his water;
to the right is the way of Gurion, grandfather of all Zion,
standing on his beautiful old head.
You grow more and more rich as you move in that direction;
you leave yourself and go to live with the diseases;
you become a river, and a house, as well as a man.
    Poor rat of 35—
you were so encumbered you couldn't begin to imagine
what a little rest could bring.
Life, the trap, it could have missed you, you could have slipped by.

I go back and forth every day now over a bridge that separates
        Riegelsville, New Jersey from Riegelsville, Pa.
The two sleepy guards barely lift their arms as they see me drive by.
In my mind are the mammoths
and the sheets of cold ice
and the men who moved up and down with the great snow.
Over there, in a swamp, the bearded Carnegie is dancing in front of his
        new library;

the workmen leave their fires and lift him up on their shoulders, singing
    in Latin;
I am already sitting there, beside the iron frog and the fountain.

THE ANGER OF AGE

The anger of age—I'll love it!
Broken teeth! Screaming
at the young!
My liver rotting
over the Talmud—
cursing the sperm wasted
on miserable dreams.

I CALLED THE WOLF JOSEPHUS

I called the wolf Josephus,
rotting in his cage,
thoughtful, greedy,
the dogs' Jew.

THERE AMONG THE DELECTABLES

I have fallen to pieces
over Romanticism.
I have fought at the back door,
dreaming of taking you *a la sinistra;*
it was my secret dream,
there among the delectables,
each with the same vice.
You are huge as an elephant.
The mistake was in assuming
you existed at all.

NO SUCCOUR!

Fishes filled the canal
and after that, stank.
For twenty years the council,
dominated by the putrid
water interest, argued
about incalculables.
You could compare *them* to fishes,
but that is only serving
the cause of vanity,
not justice.
These are men,
selfish, mystical, rich,
who know more than you
about causes and interests.
No succour!

THE HEAT RISES IN GUSTS

The heat rises in unpredictable gusts
Shaking the cords and lifting the valances.

The sofa lies against the swollen wall
Only an arm away from the window.

All this time it was not being that was a problem but tenderness.
All our talking in German was a waste, all our languages.

In the center of the room, where the weight is, stands Nietzsche the
    chopping block.
He is strapped together with unbreakable rods and locked in by bolts.

He is a monster of energy out of the nineteenth century
Redeemed by a just world.

BURST OF WIND BETWEEN BROADWAY AND THE RIVER

Between the eighth and the seventh avenue
I am hit in the face by a burst of wild air—
it is Nietzsche again, disguised as dust.
Twenty seconds we slap each other's faces,
grip hands and break each other's backs.
I sort of trot up thirty-eighth past Lerner and Bear's
looking for the dairy restaurant in which my brain was stranded.
There at the little chairs and the round tables
the rebbes read and eat.
I walk between them like a learned soul,
nodding my head and smiling,
doing the secret steps and making the signs,
following the path of authority and silence,
I and the dust, in the black soup and the herring.

TOP ROCK

This is just what I expected, the roots above the ground,
the rocks crowding out the soil, the whole universe popping in my head.
That is the heart over there
between the old leaves and the bottle,
and that is the broken neck,
and those are the shoulders reaching down to the small terrace.
    Behind the pine, through the starved needles,
Nietzsche is there preaching against redemption.
He is scolding the cripple, the hunchback and the mute;
I drag him one step at a time from his eyrie;
whatever I touch comes to pieces in my hands.
    Down below the generators are burning up the river.
The inspectors are sneaking through the weeds, disguised as fishermen.
My perverse heart is helping out, giving a little aid to the managers,
a little to the police.
My hands float on top of the water, like the fog.
I am living in both places at once.

Going down I am more like an animal
and I go sideways around the berries and the poison ivy.
After five minutes I am through the brush and practically running.
For just one second at the bottom of the hill I disappear altogether
and re-appear twenty feet away in a different clearing.
The straight hemlocks, the simple ascent,
whatever it was that made me take the one path up,

are now—for me—indistinguishable from the rest.
I will see them in the future only as a part of the general luxury
at the foot of a mountain.

COLUMBIA THE GEM

I know that body standing in the Low Library,
the right shoulder lower than the left one, the lotion sea lotion—
his hold is ended.
Now the mouths can slash away in memory
of his kisses and his stupefying lies.
Now the old Reds can walk with a little spring
in and around the beloved sarcophagi.
Now the Puerto Ricans can work up another funny America
and the frightened Germans can open their heavy doors a little.
Now the River can soften its huge heart
and move, for the first time, almost like the others,
without silence.

THE TRAITORS

It is almost three years now I have been living
in this house in the middle of Edison studying
the sycamore tree with the small bells hanging in long threads from
      the branches.

In a few months we will be moving to Raubsville, at the edge of Easton,
with hills, a canal and a river, where there will be other bodies
and other hearts to struggle with.

Now I have to do something with the bells before I leave for Raubsville.
I have to do something with the wind that goes through them
and the intimation of abandon that lies in the center of the grid.

I am living in a house with dry walls, hot air, low ceilings,
tiny baseboards, and a cellar that floods every time it rains.

Upstairs the American Family romps
over the thin floor boards, pulling us into their
harsh nest, constantly forcing us into their Hell.

Outside the huge mailboxes moan with our debts
and the Impalas and the Cougars and the Mustangs stand
around like fat camels, our only signs of wealth.

This is That Community where Friday night
we line up to buy ketchup sandwiches at McDonald's,
where we buy green bananas and concealed meat at the Acme,
and where we make our weekly journey to the shopping center.

But let us remember—at least—the traitors in our midst.
Let us remember the dogs that are deaf
and trot down the middle of the road
making the cars come to a crawl or a halt;

the old men who go into the hospital
only to come out again alive and confuse the present
with more and more of their stubborn breathing;

the small animals that pause five extra seconds (to our horror)
making their minds up before they go back again into the ground;

and they who live in imitation of some luxury out of the past,
dreaming—believe it or not—of *trains,*
dreaming (nothing to be ashamed of) of something bearded,
of something beside a dead husband—or a dead wife—to sleep by;

and they who live with the Incas (nothing to be ashamed of)
and move with deep pity through the high cities,
listening, in their ears, to the screams of the Great King
as his tongue is cut from its root and his body dismembered;

and they who bear the maze like wild rats,
shuttling back and forth on murderous nails;

and they who live again, once a month,
in the arms of a sweet friend;

and they who move in triteness down the hall of anger,
or into the kitchen, or into the garage,
choking on the truths,
begging to be listened to, begging at least to be *felt;*

and they who move like an army (nothing to be ashamed of)
through old clothes and music and macrobiotics and astrology,
and the countryside and the Orient and even old Europe and even Eleuthera;

and they who act out a ritual of cleanliness,
with friends surrounding them—sinks and toilets full of tears—
in a small apartment cluttered with doors;

and they who celebrate Earth Day, April 22,
invoking the great power of Shelley,
naming the pollutants, naming the clumsy polluters;

and they who go to New York—to a hotel—to live *in extremis,*
to try peace again with the filthy window sills;

and they who add the simple sound of motorcycles to the air,
and who, because of this, or because of asthma,
or obesity, or weird parentage, or Miztec culture or Nietzsche,
begin to find their own method of exclusion;

and they who try babies again at 40, and again at 50,
the tiny head growing smaller and smaller each time,
the love they feel growing more and more general;

and they who, because of a kind father, or a kind grandfather,
remember the principles;

and they who discover *the other side* through the quirk of stubbornness
or the quirk of myopea or the quirk of self-pity,
finding a just cause (nothing to be ashamed of) through personal weakness,
and turn to the enemy with shows of affection;

and they who go to the enemy because their hands
are sick of torture, and their mouths are sick of disguise;

and they who—whatever happens—in whose ever car they sit,
in whose ever office, in whose ever living room, in whose ever restaurant,
always know the slave from the overseer;

and they who stay, and they who go, either way
turning the cry of pain in their ears into a cry of pleasure,
turning a life that is pinched, or a life that is feared,
into a life that is loved.

DELAWARE WEST

I walk now along the mule path between the first and second locks
and come to rest in my own front yard on the Delaware River.
I am tearing one world apart and building another.
I have left the Swedes to their own dark spittle and the Poles to theirs.
I have discovered tires and bedsprings richer than anything in
      Björnstrom or Polanski.
I lift one finger to store the crazy ruins of four lifetimes
and one foot to the accumulated ash of half a century.
Under the stove, beside the broken window,
I have found the complete collection of *Orgy*.
While the light dies and the river rises
I will push the wasps aside and live in the dark
with the pregnant grandmothers, the rampant dogs
and the paralyzed strippers—
in tearful brotherhood with the grim sots
and the noisy oracles—
two long hours away from the downtown freaks
and the uptown rabbis.

PLANTING STRAWBERRIES

If this is a thing of the past,
planting strawberries on the Delaware River
and eating zucchini from my own garden,
then I will have to be buried too,
along with the beer-hall musicians
and the "startlingly beautiful sunset"
and the giant Swiss pansies,
in the ruins of Pennsylvania.
   I put the strawberries in one by one.
They look like octopuses and their feet dance in the water
as I cover them up to their necks.
They take up so much room
that I could eat an acre of them for breakfast
sitting in the dirt.
What I like best is having a garden this close to
the factories and stores of Easton.
It is like carrying a knife in my pocket!
It is like kissing in the streets!
   I would like to convert all the new spaces
back into trees and rocks.
I would like to turn the earth up after the bulldozers
have gone and plant corn and tomatoes.
I would like to guard our new property—with helmets and dogs.
I would like us to feed ourselves in the middle of their civilization.

LOOK AT US PLAY WITH OUR MEAT

Look at us play with our meat,
turning it over in the juices,
pecking at the carrot pieces.
Look at us fight for forks,
desperately looking for new silver,
the clean untarnished tines.
What a horror civilization is!
I remember walking on top of three layers,
sinking down through bed after bed,
reaching into the flint.
I remember the lopped femur,
the artistic grooves at the handle,
the club side still stained and splintered.
I remember Harry Truman signing orders,
the sun shining on his steel glasses,
the pens lined up on the velvet;
I remember him at Howard Johnsons
wolfing down the clams,
on the walls mermaids without nipples
floating in dead little pools
for the older women of America—I remember
the German mind at its peak,
rays of charity spreading in all directions,
old men in the Gobi reading Hegel,

Bushmen weeping over the sad pages of Heine,
Argentinians unpacking heavy wooden boxes of Dresden,
Japanese turning gently to the new instruments,
the winds of Leipzig and Vienna
blowing lovingly over Fuji,
the violins appearing everywhere,
the air shrieking and sighing with the new harmony.

TWO AMERICAN HAIKUS

1. Mao Tse-tung

The loose poems falling like blossoms
and the rain drops hitting the water like heads
dropping into the waste basket.

2. W. C. Fields

Gloves, gloves, and a tubular hat,
and a white carnation, and a queen of spades
and the cheeks of a president.

THE STICK OF WRATH

The love of concrete objects
led me into this deadfall.
Queen Nofret
in the sitting position.
King Zoser in water.
Virgil in wax.
—The marbles of Abu.
The kneeling woman of Baluba.
The demon Humbaba.

      I dream of the cave where Naz
      and his lovers beat their wings
      in the fire.

      I dream of the marsh where Liz
      turns her bright teeth
      on the ferns.

In the great mock spring
Lincoln comes out of the mud
like a prurient rhubarb
feeling the heat;
the banks close,
the Republicans thunder
and the hyacinths die
in their own tears.

I quit everything
at the first sign of the thaw
and worked back
to the waste places.
I thought of the bulging eyes
of the sorcerer
and like an ithyphallic
I raced along the ground,
cursing the two preposterous
images of our life,
the philosopher picking his nose
and the ape bearing a crucifix.
I drifted up to my knees
in burdocks.
I sang and breathed
in the upright position,
and with my open hands
I moved easily
through the lace and nettle.
—The sun freed me—
this I know—
the sun freed me,
drawing out poisons,
converting the ice into pools,
and laying bare our
secret tortured connections.
My head was full of light
and my blood turned,
only out of some crazy past,

some deadfall,
I kept my strange feelings
even from myself.
I bore the full guilt
of my affections—my fate,
bearing the guilt,
going round (as I do)
like a man with a weight
interested in justice.
I fought for balance and gravity—
even against the lips—
I fought for old equity,
in ignorance and nostalgia;
I fought against violence, against weakness, against perversion—
my ears rang
as I swayed with the excitement
of conflict
and my hands shook
as I moved to the points of contact.

That great love needs
good government
is the theory of Ruskin.

That loveliness
can be restored
is the theory of the sorcerer.

THE BITE

I didn't start taking myself seriously as a poet
until the white began to appear in my cheek.
All before was amusement and affection—
now, like a hare, like a hare, like a hare,
I watch the turtle lift one horrible leg
over the last remaining stile and head
for home, practically roaring with virtue.
    Everything, suddenly everything is up there in the mind,
    all the beauty of the race gone
    and my life merely an allegory.

TWO BIRDS

When I first saw this twittering thing
I knew I was in for another seige of forgiveness.
I never saw such watery eyes,
such a corrupted mouth.
God, how I am attracted to the diseased and fallen—
my house is like a hospital.
—I remember one that struck like a jay
and taught you to beware of birds.
His heart pounded with hatred—there was no pity—
and his neck jerked with a warning.
But later, much later,
he dipped his face in water, he gurgled, he preened,
and gazed at the paralyzed world with a softened eye.

They are all alike, the birds.
Rain fattens them, hunger sets them on, love dements them.
—This one lives in the dark
dreaming of its sanctuary.
Its eye follows the least light
and its mind moves in meshes.
Even its escape is weak.
Only its ecstasy, its uncontrollable fit on the singing ground,
something florid, something convulsive rolling through its wild brain
releases it.

The clumsiness and the disconnectedness are the things I stay away from.
What I like is the respect for distance and the attitude to light.
What I revere is the evening madness, the entelechy.

IT IS NOT BERENSON'S BLOOD

It is not Berenson's blood, it is not Cramer's,
it is not Carleson's. It is not Searle's.
It is not Merk's, it is not Priff's. It is not Harper's.

That delight is ended.

The waters are theirs, the bridges,
the cunning, the intimacy, even the peace;
but not the blood.

I am dividing my life up.
I am separating pleasure from disease and kindness from humiliation.
I am becoming a prince of ashes.
I have learned to nourish fire, to love oxygen, to live with the shovel.
I have come to respect the smoke, to honor the chain.
Day after day I free the living coals.
And shake away the dross. And feed the flame.
It is my life.

DOG IN THE HOUSE

On Long Island in 1951 I fought against bats for hours
and ended up with a little pile of bodies on the dining-room table,

and I have killed spiders inside the house so large
they bleed to death from their wounds like mammals,

and I lived for a whole year once
with a parasitical fox under my back porch,

and I have been horrified enough by baby birds in the attic
and live squirrels in the wall,

and I have had to slam the front door against dogs
and wait like a prisoner in my own living room,

so when it snows I look very carefully at the tracks
to see which ones hang back and which come close,
knowing what exhaustion does to animals.

In humans when it comes there is no control in the heart;
we spend our time in remorse
and weep at the sight of our frozen clothes
and look at our feet with pity.

We lose our thoughts,
we turn to phantasy and contortion,
we walk without leverage
and fall down from confusion.

The rest of our lives we spend in front of a fire
remembering our cold bodies
and the frightening steps we took to save them.

IN CARPENTER'S WOODS

This is a corner of heaven here,
the moss growing under the leaves,
the rocks cropping up like small graves under the trees,
the old giants rotting in the shade.
I used to come here every Sunday
to stand on the bridge and look at the bird-watchers.
Once I made love in the dead brush
and slept impaled on the thorns, too tired to move;
once I gave myself up to the *New York Times*
and buried myself in sections a whole afternoon;
once I played football with the radicals
while the sun and the rain fought for control.
    At the bottom of the hill where the trees give way to grass
a creek runs through a silent picnic ground
almost a mile away from any access.
Here the neighborhood dogs broke into their runs
at the first threat of authority.
Here the exhibitionists came out in the open
after the long morning with the squirrels and flickers.
Here the Jehovah's Witnesses lay down their arms
and gathered quietly around the tables.
—Without knowing the name or the reason
I gave myself up to vertigo;
I lay for hours with my eyes closed listening to the great sounds

coming in from Germantown;

I loved the ground so much that I had to hold on to the grass for balance.

    I can tell you that where those two girls go carefully over the stones,
and where that civilized man and his son
pick up loose wood for the fireplace
was, for three years, my refuge.
I can tell you that I have spent half a lifetime hunting for relief,
that in the simplest locations, in libraries,
in drug stores, in bus stations—
as well as under stone bridges and on hillsides—
I have found places to wait and think.
I tell you that world is as large as the one you sigh and tremble over;
that it is also invulnerable and intricate and pleasurable;
that it has a serious history;
that it was always there, from the beginning.

EROICA

Forgive me for being alone.
I'm breaking skulls like I used to
to get at the brain.
Now I am drinking fragments of memory,
now I am sucking on idle nerve cells.
This is Haydn here, who belonged to Carl Rosenbaum,
he is full of holes;
and that is Emmanuel Swedenborg
under the eighteenth century wig.
    There used to be dozens of us here;
now, beside myself, there are only a few others.
We're crazy, aren't we?
What gives us away?
I watch the president's party
wave goodbye;
I watch learned men and women
sit down on dirty little rugs
and I go back to my skulls in peace.
    "A jet of fire, a rain of stars in the night . . ."
Old Rolland and I are paying tribute to Beethoven.
". . . the voice of Death is drowned in the roars of Joy,
in the rush of the Revolution mob
demolishing the Bastilles and leaping over the tombs."
He was a skull-master too, Beethoven.

He knew how to widen the opening,
he knew how to lift the juices to his lips,
he knew all the highways and byways.
True, he was a bastard.
True, the screams of the poor reached his ears in a strange way.
True, he made a fetish of morality.
—Ah, we would differ on pity,
and I could never beat my breast like he did,
but I would give something to walk round the ramparts with him,
even to argue with him about Klopstock *und* Goethe.
I would love to reason with him about the *ubermensch.*
I would love to swap tales about our covenants with injustice.
I would love to fight with him over the soul.
   I'd like to hear him thunder,
with all his opaqueness;
I would be still, sometimes, for that one.
For that one I would drag out my discarded rug, and listen.

FROM THE PENNSYLVANIA SIDE

The weeds are out,
the flowering heads, the prickles,
I can walk with safety again.
I study the roadsides and fences
with secret pleasure;
all the stragglers and drifters
are blooming peacefully;
no one in the whole county will disturb them.

It isn't daytime yet for the chained dogs
and I am able to sneak past them for the first time
without a sound.
I smile at the floating hair
taking me seriously as a hillside
and the sticky barbs mistaking me for a sheep.
Like a loyal friend
I shift my leg to let the small teeth
get a good grip on my socks and shoe laces
and kick my toes in the mud
to liberate the sleepers.

At 6 A.M. I wash my eyes with dew
as Dante did at the foot of Purgatory
and fill my lungs with a little morning air
to clear my brain of Hell.

74

The Riegel Paper Company
is all I can see from where I sit.
Its stone chimneys and rusted machinery
belie its subtle connection
with Chase Manhattan and New England Life.
Inside hatchet men from International
are forcing the career men out
and the whole valley is trembling with bankruptcy.
Down the road the People's Dump
still takes whatever the rich Hog rejects.
There is enough free paper there
for the artists on both sides of the river.

I put my head on the ground
and lie there thinking.
For years I have been trying to figure out which I hate the most,
the House Beautiful with microwave ovens and high-heat incinerators
or the House Ugly with leaky stoves
and plastic bags spilling out over the sidewalk.
Across the river the milk run from Trenton
works its way up to Riegelsville, New Jersey.
It will take a whole morning
to maneuver four boxcars onto the siding
and three full days to unload them.
I will pass them once in the morning and once in the afternoon
on my own run into New Jersey.
I will slow down to look at the faded symbols
and read the signs.
Overhead the birds will pass obscure seeds

through their stomachs
and whatever the birds don't take the wind will.

At 8 o'clock I will go into the Cup and Saucer for breakfast.
The moody owner will stare resentfully into his television set,
the tired women will fall asleep over their coffee
and the heavy men will bend quietly over their eggs and bread.
The struggle for air and water will be forgotten
at the little tables;
no one in the room will have to fight for sunlight
or search for space;
they will be able to rest themselves—for thirty minutes—
before they go back again to their small trucks and their houses.

TURNING INTO A POND

All I need is one foot in the mud
to keep my sanity.
That way the water snakes can swim through my blood
and the greedy pickerel can hide
under my leaves.
All I have to do is fall asleep in the water
and let the yellow lights turn from gold to brown
as I sink to the bottom.
When it rains I can lie face down in the lilies
and let the naked couples rest their tired legs on my back.
When it gets dark I can sing to them about insanity
and compare my community to theirs.
I will release information softly,
using a deep voice for emphasis,
telling them one thing at a time.
At night I will slow down
and drift with the zooplankton.
I will dream about Voltaire and his white feet,
about Mozart and his hands.
The large mammals will waddle down to the shore
and drop their heads into the water.
The dragonfly will pull in its murderous lip
and the fisher spider will rest on its line.
In a century or two the beavers will turn me into a meadow
and my muddy wife will walk over my chest listening for cattails.

We will be so far apart it will take us weeks to reach each other.
Going by road you will be able to point me out when you get to Two
    Bridges,
in back of Penn Run, in Indiana County.
The weeds and grasses are beginning to struggle for attention;
the water is turning warm; we are going into April.

A Note on the Author

Gerald Stern was born in Pittsburgh in 1925 and educated at the University of Pittsburgh and Columbia University. He lived, in the fifties, in New York City and Europe, stretching out his World War II G.I. Bill, tutoring, and teaching high school English in Glasgow, Scotland. He has taught at a number of colleges and universities, including Temple University, the University of Pittsburgh, and Sarah Lawrence College, and, since 1982, he has been on the faculty of the Writers' Workshop at the University of Iowa. He has received many grants and awards, including the Guggenheim Fellowship and two National Endowment for the Arts Creative Writing grants. His book *Lucky Life* was the Lamont Poetry Selection in 1977, he received the Bess Hokin Award from *Poetry* in 1980, and he won the Melville Cane Award in 1981 for *The Red Coal*. In 1982 *The Paris Review* gave him the Bernard F. Conners Poetry Prize for his long poem "Father Guzman."